Arts

OF GREAT BRITAIN

SELECTED SHORTER

POEMS

WITHDRAWN FROM THE POETRY LIBRARY

SELECTED SHORTER
POEMS
JAMES REANEY
EDITED BY GERMAINE WARKENTIN

EDITORIAL

Copyright © 1975 by James Reaney
Introduction Copyright © 1975 by Germaine Warkentin
All rights reserved.
No part of this book may be reproduced or transmitted in any form by
any means, electronic or mechanical, including photocopying and
recording, information storage and retrieval systems, without
permission in writing from the publisher, except by a reviewer who
may quote brief passages in a review.
ISBN 88878-063-X
First published by Press Porcepic, 70 Main Street, Erin, Ontario in
August of 1975 with the assistance of the Canada Council and the
Ontario Arts Council.
Printed in Canada.
1   2   3   4   5   79   78   77   76   75

Distribution:

CANADA	U.S.A.	U.K. & EUROPE
Burns & MacEachern Ltd.	Press Porcepic Ltd.	Books Canada Ltd.
62 Railside Road	70 Main Street	1 Bedford Road
Don Mills, Ontario	Erin, Ontario	London N2
M3A 1A6	N0B 1T0	England

Canadian Shared Cataloguing in Publication Data

Reaney, James, 1926 -
    Selected shorter poems / by
James Reaney.

I. Title.
PS8535.E12A6 1975 811.54
PR9199.3.R43A6 1975
ISBN: 0-88878-063-X

CONTENTS

Books by James Reaney

The Red Heart
A Suit of Nettles
Twelve Letters to a Small Town
The Killdeer and Other Plays
The Dance of Death in London, Ontario
Colours in the Dark
Listen to the Wind
Poems
Masks of Childhood
Apple Butter and Other Plays
The Donnellys
    I Sticks and Stones
    II The St. Nicholas Hotel, Wm. Donnelly Proprietor
    III Handcuffs
All the Bees and All the Keys
Selected Shorter Poems
Selected Longer Poems

INTRODUCTION

James Reaney's dramas have been acted all across Canada, and his epic trilogy *The Donnellys* (1973-75) packed the Tarragon Theatre in Toronto as its parts were produced one by one. But as both the substance and vision of his plays testify, Reaney is a fine poet as well. He has been writing since the forties and by now his non-dramatic verse stands as a major achievement beside his plays, and in poetry makes him the peer of Scott, Birney, Layton, Avison, and Purdy.

The audience for Reaney's poetry has always been an unusual one. At its centre is a core of passionately convinced readers like myself who find his poems among the most richly satisfying written in Canada. At its outer edge are enthusiasts who know only the dozen pieces, mostly from his early work, that are regularly anthologized, and who think that he has written little else. Between these two groups are a lot of puzzled readers, some of them fellow poets, who find his central images naive, resent his bookishness, and are dubious about the influence mythopoeic criticism is supposed to have had on his work. One thing is sure: Reaney is a truly mythopoeic poet; his poems do not record the world for us, they re-make the world on an entirely visionary model. To read Reaney is not to read a book of poems, it is to enter a new cosmos bursting with verbal energy, yet full of familiar forms — children, geese, farmhouses — that are transmuted by the poet's intelligence and simplicity into symbols of the whole world of man.

In one respect Reaney is unlike many other English-Canadian poets: he does not write much about nature, nor does he use it as a metaphor. Wherever there is a garden in his poems, there tends to be a city as well, and even his recurrent image for the geographic fabric of Canada is a vagrant old lady, Granny Crack. Thus, though his poetry is anything but political, he in fact writes mostly about society. In his earliest poems that society had only one inhabitant, the solitary child of *The Red Heart* (1949):

> All things are voiceless save the sound
> Of some plums falling through the summer air
> Straight to the ground.
> And there is no listener, no hearer . . .
> Save a child who, lolling
> Among the trunks and old featherticks
> That fill the room where he was born,
> Hears them in his silent dreaming . . .

One poem, "Play-box", written even before *The Red Heart*, shows us the child and his world in a form we are to meet frequently in Reaney's work. "Play-box" is a dramatic monologue spoken by a child who expects to be orphaned. Composedly he plans to "camp in a fence-corner/ And be independent awhile," and assembles the treasures of his play-box to take along. By the end of the poem the box has become the child's winter habitation, where he lies hidden with his lantern, surrounded by the relics of his past. In the early poetry the poet never emerges from this hibernation. "Play-box" ends with the child's recognition that the possible home in a fence-corner is a dream; his real destination is the orphanage.

Years later, The Red Heart was to find its dramatic counterpart in Reaney's play, Colours in the Dark, produced at Stratford in 1967. The Red Heart is itself a kind of play-box, and Colours in the Dark draws on many of its poems to compose, in a kind of vaudeville, a spiritual biography based on the poet's life and works. Colours in the Dark shows the lost child becoming an adult. He is not, however, an orphaned and bitter grown-up, but a father himself, who, through a natural process of thinking, questioning, and recognition (and helped by many unexpected friends), finally grows into joyous possession of his own identity. What Dave Godfrey calls the wonderful health of Reaney's world is shown powerfully in a lyric which is part of the same evolution, and tells of a father who is seeking, and eventually finds, his lost son:

> Oh Life in Death! my bonny nursling
> Merry drummer in the nut brown coffin,
> With vast wings outspread I float
> Looking and looking over the empty sea
>
> And there! in the — on the rolling death
> Rattling a dried out gourd
> Floated the mysterious cradle
> Filled with a source.
>
> I push the shore and kingdom to you,
> Oh winter walk with seedpod ditch:
> I touch them to the floating child
> And lo! Cities and gardens, shepherds and smiths.

Despite its optimism, Reaney's poetry has a tough-minded and satirical streak. Satire is foremost in his major long poem, A Suit of Nettles (1958). In the shorter poems, there is satiric potential, not merely in the poet's attacks on a "so-so civilization" (see "The Man Hunter", "Winnipeg Seen As a Body of Time and Space", and "Starling with a Split Tongue") but in the very energy of the poetry itself, no matter what its subject. Reaney writes about a hummingbird:

> The hum of an approaching christening mob!
> The hanging still in the air with so much motion
> He flies with wings of air in an air of feathers!
> The hanging still in the air with so much motion
>
> The hollow twig that transports flowers to his blood
> The barn of flowers pressed in a jumping ounce

No song is needed when one is a song
The barn of flowers pressed in a jumping ounce

and his poems, after an early period of aestheticism seem to behave with the same sharp energy and excitement. Their symbolism is rich (Reaney's literary ancestry can be traced through Yeats and Blake back to Spenser), their verbal intricacy is the result of exacting craftsmanship and great wit, and they approach the reader both visually and musically.

Reaney sometimes illustrates his poems himself, and regards printed layout as an important part of their effect. Comparing the early poem "The Gramaphone" and the more recent emblem "The Tree", we can see how richly he has developed this kind of experimentation while preserving and transforming the special elements of his symbolic world. Reaney is a musician also, and his poems often hint at ballad or song form; he has written that it was learning to accommodate his verse to the demands of a composer (as he did in 1953 when he wrote the libretto for John Beckwith's chamber opera *Night-Blooming Cereus*) that ultimately taught him poetic craftsmanship. Among Canadian poets he is the technical virtuoso, a fact that accounts both for the *élan* of his non-dramatic verse and for many of the delights his major dramas present for an actor.

I began by saying that Reaney writes about society. Certainly his poems and dramas are suffused by a vision of the perfected society all men long to live in. But they are filled as well with the texture of his own country's history, whether seen satirically, as in his version of Pierre Falcon's song:

Governor thought himself a king.
He wished an iron rod to swing.
Like a lofty lord he tries to act.
    Bad luck, old chap!
    A bit too hard you whacked!

When we went galloping, galloping by
Governor thought that he would try
For to chase and frighten us Bois-Brûlés.
    Catastrophe!
    Dead on the ground he lay.

or more poignantly, as in the same poem:

Far away and dear, spunky old and early poet
I wish I could sing the praises of the Neon People
To You.

If his shorter poems deal with the self as primal inhabitant of that society, it is Reaney's longer poems which, appropriately, step back to look at life as it is lived in the community as a whole. Two later volumes will present these poems: first, *A Suit of Nettles*, and second, *Selected Longer Poems*, a collection of Reaney's longer sequences centring on *Twelve Letters to a Small Town*. The selected shorter poems in this book all lead to these later works just as the pebble, dewdrop, string and straw of "The Yellow-Bellied Sapsucker" all signify in special ways the patterning which for Reaney seems an inherent part of existence:

> The pebble was a mountain that took years to climb
> The dewdrop was all reality itself
> The string was the pathway to Heaven
> The straw formed God's name
> The groundhog meant that death was laughter.

"To what journey's end?" writes Reaney doubtfully; "perhaps some hayloft/ with the rain beating down on the owly roof," but then muses,

> The mountain is a pebble in your hand
> The abyss of Space is a dewdrop
> Heaven Road lies ravelled in your pocket
> Time's cloud of moments is a rain drop . . .
> The holy Ghost is your wife or husband,
> Shakespeare, your whistle,
> And the thousand eyes of fancy make each idle stare
> Possible breakthrough to the perfect.

Reaney's poems and plays compose the "nine mused and pleated winnowing fan of wisdom" that challenges us to share this vision.

Germaine Warkentin
Victoria College
Summer, 1975.

A Note on the Text

Readers are referred to the original Note and Acknowledgements in *Poems*, from which the order and texts and line numbering have been taken. But reviewers are asked to note that "The Butterfly and the Moth" on page 68 is deliberately inverted. The drawing for that poem is by Tony Urquhart, and is reproduced by permission of the owner. The drawings for *Twelve Letters to a Small Town* and the emblem poems are by James Reaney. The text from *Sticks and Stones* is as it appears in *Poems*. This was taken from an early version of the play before it had undergone its workshop evolution. Readers might be interested to compare the two versions.

Play-box

If my step-father doesn't get much better
I don't suppose he will.
I will camp in a fence-corner
And be independent awhile.
The fence-corner where Effie
Lost her string of pearls
In an April-puddle
But in June we found them all again.
There I shall take my spotted ring
And the wool-blanket hemmed with red.   10
I shall set my clock up in a corner
Pears and grapes on its lid.
Also the corduroy suit
And the scarf with the purple bars
A pot of rouge in case I should ever go out.
The Illustrated News I'll get
And read it all the day
In June I'll eat wild strawberries
July there's a field of peaze.
In August the Duchess apples are ripe.   20

By that time I'll probably have
My play-box filled with old toys and scrap-books.
And poor dead butterfly wings.
No more hoeing for me
No more scrubbing of floors
No more holding of wood
While another chops dangerously near.
No more medicining horses
With their heads tied up to the roof
Nor any more calvings to watch   30
Kittens to drown or attempts to murther me.

When the ruts are white in Cardwell's Bush
As the Pork Street ballad goes
And the grain's all in that fall.
When the field-mice are all boarded
In the barn among the hay,
I shall take one walk across the fields.
Where the killdeers lie.
Lie buried and my father's horse in a corner
That we named after a judge.   40
And there are cow-horns sprinkled.

I shall shut myself up in my play-box hall.
Shut the lid; sleep the winter through.
With my toy green lantern for light.
They'll find me in the spring.

If I go to the orphanage
I will always dream of this . . .
My possible home in the fence-corner.
A spotted ring, a butterfly wing.
A green lantern's light.   50

1945

Faces and the Drama in a Cup of Tea

The cup had the outlines of a cup
In a lantern-slide.
And it was filled with Congou tea
What did it mean this cup of tea?
Perhaps the law of eight times seven
Will change some day.
Some teacher's cheek
Will blush in realized mistake.
It will be a sort of city-sunset on her cheek
Reflected in the window of a seamstress.   10
She will say:
The whole universe lies on a window-sill,
A speck of sulphur or a slowly dying pin,
Bloodying in rust.
A speck of sulphur on a shelf
A dying pin turning to bloodred rust.
Then there will come a strange deny of time.
Various street-cries embroidered in the mist.

1946

12

Kodak (1927)

Miss ffrench and Brownshoes
(For many years we gave Brownshoes
Large benefits of doubt).
Have come to see my garden.
Noiselessly, they walk
The winding worms of air
That are its paths.
They pat the childish sunflowers
Regard the fragments of Mary's Dress
The Forget-me-nots display,   10
And swoom low over the moss-roses.
Miss ffrench is dressed in the fashion of the year.
A narrow egyptian frock.
Brownshoes' moustache is like
Two gold-fish, leaping for his nose.
Officiously, like a little widow, the orchard-grass
Has wept its dew upon their shoes.
The gold thread that hems Miss ffrench's dress
Seems to say in Morse, ahem.
Her shoes are moving up and down   20
As breasts with breath.
They have their camera.
No one sits in its gloomy parlour
Of pleated walls.
No wind stirs or ghost stalks,
Except the very large eye of God.
Miss ffrench makes God wink
("You'd better let me take it this time
You're too nervous")
And all my garden . . .   30
And all my garden stands suddenly imprisoned
Within her pleated den.

1946

A Prayer

Water obeys the rules set down
Of creeks and rivers, oceans and fountains
Of china and glass and crockery
But I, O Lord, only Thy Dish
In which you apparently placed me;
A Dish of Desires. Which are
Gold wallpaper, cake and tea
Someone playing or singing
An Oboe
Or a Banjo   10
A white-toothed piano.
Die for me if you must, dear God
But please keep these things overflowing.

1947

The Gramaphone

Upon the lake
At Gramaphone
A beastly bird
Sits on the bank
And dips its beak
Of sharpened bone
Into a haunted
Tank
That ripples with an eternal stone.

When the ladies descend the stairs,   10
Some eat their fans
And others comb their hair.
But Miss Mumblecrust
Picks up that beastly bird
And dips its beak
Into that round lake
That ripples with eternal stone
And dips its beak of sharpened bone
Into a pool of a young man singing
"I'm all alone   20
By the telephone!"

1947

14

Tarzan jad guru

Young muscular Edwardian
  Swings through trees,
  Stops carnage at Karnak,
  Whole trains at Windhoek,
  Dances waltzes simianese.
Lord Greystoke jad guru.

A dumb yellow drum
  Hangs down from the night.
  For the rite of the Dum Dum
  Come the cousin apes.
  He who could wear Bond Street   10
  And opera capes
  Prefers loin cloths of
  Impeccable cut.
Lady Jane Greystoke jad guru.

Mazumba waves his spear!
  Oh the white beach and the green palms!
  Stygian night between the ears!
  Oh Prince of slaughter do not bungle
  My jugular vein within the jungle,   20
  And springboks flee across the plains
  From apes with silver headed canes.
Edward VII jad guru!

1947

* The seventh of the Tarzan books has a language Edgar
Rice Burroughs invented for the prehistoric people
Tarzan meets on the other side of a mysterious African
lake: "jad guru" means "the Terrible". Also, Tarzan's
real name is Lord Greystoke.

The Birth of Venus

I
In and underneath
The warm sea breathing
Up and down
Feverish-breasted with waves
White legs of papier-mache assemble.
A torso of pink rubber
Has holes for long wooden arms
A wool and marble head
And room for the giant lover
Expectant upon the peacock-spotted marble shore.   10

II
Apples fall like desultory tennis
In the dark orchard where chaste stout trees
Stiffly fondle fondly
Whose roots flow like purple brooks
Over the ground-hog hollow earth.
We lie so close
Upon the grass
The gunpowder in our thick-twigged hearts
Dreams of the fiercest command
So that our two hearts rush out   20
Like two red star-shells bursting from
The toothless mouths of cannon
Killing each other instantly
Among the demisemiquaver cricket cries
In the hush between the falls of pears
Like moons and stars in a green sky
Appear upon the green-needled lawn.
And sad old trees with bellies
Watch us
Until there is only one shadow between us   30
Until we have swallowed each other's
Fish-eyed soul
Until the red hair and branches
That lace and lightning the night
Of our limbs
Enmeshes entangles
Inextricably
In one explosive
Fated glow
While we lie in each other   40
Like one river
Drowning face down
In another river.

III
In the brown darkness
Of the earth beneath us
Lies the dead groundhog
Who died in bed.
Here in the starless fog
The subterranean branches
Of the ancient orchard   50
Wage battle
For night-soil and corpses.
These skull-sized apples
Mean the late-discovered shroud
Of the murthered child
Transformed into a hundred
Red gouts and gobbets
Of yellow wood and red blood.
So beneath our counterpane
Country of march-pane joy   60
Lie hate and death, battle
And conflicting rusty saws and
Orange-speckled swords.
From this love
This death of death
Up seventy gray stairs
Runs the eager messenger
To hang out
The very red eye of death again itself.

1947

17

Winter's Tales

As planets love an ancient star
And move in far dances round its fire
So the farmer and his children sit
About their stove whose flamey wit
Giggles in red and yellow laughter
Like a small sun caught in iron armour.
When outside the winter winds are loud
Close by their summery stove they crowd.

Through the windows they may see
The cold wind herd a river of snow   10
Beneath the moon, across the land
All locked in Winter's frog-cold hand.
And sometimes the wind does shove
Between the window sill and window
Beneath the door and across the floor
White whisks and brooms of snow.
Through every little crack
At the front door and the back
Came the soft white hands of snow
That, with its heat, the stove does smash   20
Into a harmless flat thin splash.
Then down the chimney the wind came
Till the fire seemed somewhat lame
Until someone poked at it
Or put on another stick
And it blazed up again.
The wind, the cold snow and the rain
Could not put that stove out
But in a furious dance
They kept a safe distance   30
Always beyond the window pane
So that the farmer and his children
By the stove sitting tight
Only heard the wind and never felt
Its sharp cold bite.
Then the farmer told them stories
That his father had told him
Of the massacre at Lucan
Where the neighbors killed all of the McKilligans dead
Except one little boy who crawled under a bed;   40
Of the little boy carried off by a bear
And, "a ball of fire leaped out of the earth
At him and vanished into thin air.

18

Your grandmother saw
Tecumseh's head on a pole;
Had also dined with him once
And when she looked into her soup
At the bottom of the bowl
She saw a groundhog's paw.
And Indian Sal who picked flax   50
And drank vinegar and had attacks
And Granny Crack
Who wandered the countryside
With seven petticoats to her back.
And Towser Smith who
When it rained for five days in a row
Went out and shook his fist at the sky,
His fist at God in the sky.
And how when I was a child
You stood at the table   60
And ate off a pie-tin
Not sit on chairs and eat off a plate
As you do now.
And how bricks and mortar
Couldn't keep her from marrying him.''
Then the farmer and his children grow drowsy
With the heat of the fire so blowsy
And the stories their father tells them
Of the good and bad old days
Grow shorter and shorter   70
Till the fire alone seems to talk.
Its ripening red now seeming
A massive convulsive giant's heart
A Robin's red breast.
A sunset in summer,
The rising and large Harvest Moon
When she walks out of the east, —
All these things seems the fire
Which, with their father's stories
Will long be remembered   80
And protect them from growing old.
Winter's tales that like gold
In the purses of their hearts
Will ring and shine forever
Warming them in the long winter's cold.

1949

The Canadian

How sad it is, this winter farmhouse parlour
Coloured like the bindings of religious books,
Dull green, brown and dingy maroon,
And the stove as black as a bible.
And Grandfather in his picture looks
Reproachful, as if to say
You can't sit here reading!
Isn't there anything you can do?
Did I clear this farm for this?
To which I reply: It's Sunday   10
And I'll loll in idleness here
As long as I want to, Grandpa Dear,
With occasional glances at a treatise on law;
(Your terrific success at chopping up wood,
Grandpa,
Has enabled your son to go to Osgoode.)
Besides which I'm reading Foxe's *Martyrs*,
How they put Saint Jude in a hollow log
And sawed that log in seven pieces.
There's a very good illustration   20
In which they're making a seventh saw.
I yawn and look at the clock
Or the picture of a collie-dog
Lying on his master's grave
At which I've often cried,
Or the print of the Fathers of Confederation
Or a view of the Windmills at Boom
Things that pass for decoration
In this dowdy stuffy room
Where I sit in the centre of the Christmas vacation   30
Alone, with only the ticking clock
For Company, and the fire and the wind outside.

The frost upon the windowpanes
Seems South Sea Islands there
Whose still and stiff white palms of ice
No South Wind rearranges
With warm soft arms of air.
This stove I'm sitting by
With the heat of its orange fire
Makes this room seem shifted   40
Out of this wintry season
To a stifled hot July.
I get up and hands in pockets
Look through the icy window
Upon the sea of snow

Whose white and chilly waves
Have drowned all summer's sailors
The green leaves and the oriole's song
The bee-speckled winds
The black moth in the long grass,   50
All these lie in their graves
With the long shadows of an eight o'clock sunset
With the vanished jewels of summer dew
All somewhere beneath this wig of snow
Where in the gray sky the feeble sun
Low in the sky to the south is hung
And where, bottled up in this warm windless dungeon,
I watch from this parlour window.

I long for hot lands
Where cocoa trees grow   60
That bend in the trade wind breeze
That has flowed through gay bands
Of precious spice plants
And orange and lemon trees
Where birds fly who never leave
Sadly for the South
Where flowers grow that never grieve
With terror of the frost
And there are palms
Beneath whose green spokes   70
Chant and dance the heathen folks
Who have no laws
And whose clothes
Are the blessed winds that surround them
And perhaps a feather
And whose consciences
So fattened in us by this weather
Have never found them.

So I long in this dark parlour,
Dull green, brown and maroon,   80
The colour of starling feathers,
This stuffy dingy room.
These dreams of tropical weathers!
My grim grandfather!
The Fathers of Confederation!
These windows embossed
With a mocking white imitation
Of what I wish for, in frost.

1949

SELECTIONS FROM
THE RED HEART-1949

The Plum Tree

The plums are like blue pendulums
That thrum the gold-wired winds of summer.
In the opium-still noon they hang or fall,
The plump, ripe plums.
I suppose my little sister died
Dreaming of looking up at them,
Of lying beneath that crooked plum tree,
That green heaven with blue stars pied.
In this lonely haunted farmhouse
All things are voiceless save the sound   10
Of some plums falling through the summer air
Straight to the ground.
And there is no listener, no hearer
For the small thunders of their falling
(Falling as dead stars rush to a winter sea)
Save a child who, lolling
Among the trunks and old featherticks
That fill the room where he was born,
Hears them in his silent dreaming
On a dark engraving to a fairy-tale forlorn.   20
Only he hears their intermittent soft tattoo
Upon the dry, brown summer ground
At the edge of the old orchard.
Only he hears, and farther away,
Some happy animal's slow, listless moo.

The Sundogs

I saw the sundogs barking
On either side of the Sun
As he was making his usual will
And last testament
In a glorious vestment.
And the sundogs cried,
"Bow wow!
We'll make a ring
Around the moon
And children, seeing it, will say: 10
Up there they play Farmer in the Dell
And the moon like the cheese stands still.
Bow wow!
We shall drown the crickets,
Set the killdeer birds crying,
Send shingles flying,
And pick all the apples
Ripe or not.
Our barking shall overturn
Hencoops and rabbit-hutches,   20
Shall topple over privies
With people inside them,
And burn with invisible,
Oh, very invisible!
Flames
In each frightened tree.
Whole branches we'll bite off
And for the housewife's sloth
In not taking them in
We'll drag her sheets and pillow cases   30
Off the fence
And dress up in them

And wear them thin.
And people will say
Both in the country
And in the town
It falls in pails
Of iron nails.
We'll blow the curses
Right back into the farmer's mouths   40
As they curse our industry
And shake their fists,
For we will press the oats
Close to the ground,
Lodge the barley,
And rip open the wheat stooks.
We shall make great faces
Of dampness appear on ceilings
And blow down chimneys
Till the fire's lame.   50
With the noise of a thousand typewriters
We shall gallop over the roofs of town.
We are the Sun's animals.
We stand by him in the West
And ready to obey
His most auburn wish
For Rain, Wind and Storm."

The Crow

A fool once caught a crow
That flew too near even for his stone's throw.
Alone beneath a tree
He examined the black flier
And found upon its sides
Two little black doors.
He opened both of them.
He expected to see into
Perhaps a little kitchen
With a stove, a chair,   10
A table and a dish
Upon that table.
But he only learned that crows
Know a better use for doors than to close
And open, and close and open
Into dreary, dull rooms.

The Red Heart

The only leaf upon its tree of blood,
My red heart hangs heavily
And will never fall loose,
But grow so heavy
After only a certain number of seasons
(Sixty winters, and fifty-nine falls,
Fifty-eight summers, and fifty-seven springs)
That it will bring bough
Tree and the fences of my bones
Down to a grave in the forest   10
Of my still upright fellows.

So does the sun hang now
From a branch of Time
In this wild fall sunset.
Who shall pick the sun
From the tree of Eternity?
Who shall thresh the ripe sun?
What midwife shall deliver
The Sun's great heir?
It seems that no one can,   20
And so the sun shall drag
Gods, goddesses and parliament buildings,
Time, Fate, gramaphones and Man
To a gray grave
Where all shall be trampled
Beneath the dancing feet of crowds
Of other still-living suns and stars.

The Royal Visit

When the King and the Queen came to Stratford
Everyone felt at once
How heavy the Crown must be.
The Mayor shook hands with their Majesties
And everyone presentable was presented
And those who weren't have resented
It, and will
To their dying day.
Everyone had almost a religious experience
When the King and Queen came to visit us   10
(I wonder what they felt!)
And hydrants flowed water in the gutters
All day.
People put quarters on the railroad tracks
So as to get squashed by the Royal Train
And some people up the line at Shakespeare
Stayed in Shakespeare, just in case—
They did stop too,
While thousands in Stratford
Didn't even see them   20
Because the Engineer didn't slow down
Enough in time.
And although,
But although we didn't see them in any way
(I didn't even catch the glimpse
The teacher who was taller did
Of a gracious pink figure)
I'll remember it to my dying day.

The Upper Canadian

I wish I had been born beside a river
Instead of this round pond
Where the geese white as pillows float
In continual circles
And never get out.

Sometimes I wish that I
Hadn't been born in this dull township
Where fashion, thought and wit
Never penetrate,
Unless the odd quotation from *Handy Andy*   10
Is really what I demand,
What I want.

The river, the railroad,
And His Majesty's Highways
Number Seven and Eight
Go through town
And never are the same again.
But this pond and I
Go through and become
Nothing different.   20
Now if I went away
And left this little lake,
If I struck out for the railroad and the river,
I might lose my way.
I would have to win a scholarship
Or build a Punch and Judy Show.
I'd better not,
I'd better stay.

And watch the darning-needle flies
Fly and glitter in the shining wind   30
Of summer by this pond.
At night I'll read
The Collected Works of William Shakespeare
By an empty stove
And think at least there's this
Although I'll never see it acted.
I'll hear the rain outside
And, if it's August,
A cricket's sharp chirp in the pantry.
I won't go away   40
Unless it rains and rains
Making the pond so large
That it joins the river,
But it never will.
I shall always sit here in this hovel
Weeping perhaps over an old Victorian novel
And hear the dingy interwinding tunes
Of country rain and wind
And lame fires of damp wood.
Especially shall I hear that starved cricket   50
My mind, that thinks a railway ticket
Could save it from its enclosed, cramped quality.
That mind where thoughts float round
As geese do round a pond
And never get out.

Antichrist as a Child

When Antichrist was a child
He caught himself tracing
The capital letter A
On a window sill
And wondered why
Because his name contained no A.
And as he crookedly stood
In his mother's flower-garden
He wondered why she looked so sadly
Out of an upstairs window at him.   10
He wondered why his father stared so
Whenever he saw his little son
Walking in his soot-coloured suit.
He wondered why the flowers
And even the ugliest weeds
Avoided his fingers and his touch.
And when his shoes began to hurt
Because his feet were becoming hooves
He did not let on to anyone
For fear they would shoot him for a monster.   20
He wondered why he more and more
Dreamed of eclipses of the sun,
Of sunsets, ruined towns and zeppelins,
And especially inverted, upside down churches.

The Katzenjammer Kids

With porcupine locks
And faces which, when
More closely examined,
Are composed of measle-pink specks,
These two dwarf imps,
The Katzenjammer Kids,
Flitter through their Desert Island world.
Sometimes they get so out of hand
That a blue Captain
With stiff whiskers of black wicker   10
And an orange Inspector
With a black telescope
Pursue them to spank them
All through that land
Where cannibals cut out of brown paper
In cardboard jungles feast and caper,
Where the sea's sharp waves continually
Waver against the shore faithfully
And the yellow sun above is thin and flat
With a collar of black spikes and spines   20
To tell the innocent childish heart that
It shines
And warms (see where she stands and stammers)
The dear fat mother of the Katzenjammers.
Oh, for years and years she has stood
At the window and kept fairly good
Guard over the fat pies that she bakes
For her two children, those dancing heartaches.
Oh, the blue skies of that funny paper weather!
The distant birds like two eyebrows close together!   30
And the rustling paper roar
Of the waves
Against the paper sands of the paper shore!

The School Globe

Sometimes when I hold
Our faded old globe
That we used at school
To see where oceans were
And the five continents,
The lines of latitude and longitude,
The North Pole, the Equator and the South Pole—
Sometimes when I hold this
Wrecked blue cardboard pumpkin
I think: here in my hands   10
Rest the fair fields and lands
Of my childhood
Where still lie or still wander
Old games, tops and pets;
A house where I was little
And afraid to swear
Because God might hear and
Send a bear
To eat me up;
Rooms where I was as old   20
As I was high;
Where I loved the pink clenches,
The white, red and pink fists
Of roses; where I watched the rain
That Heaven's clouds threw down
In puddles and rutfuls
And irregular mirrors
Of soft brown glass upon the ground.
This school globe is a parcel of my past,
A basket of pluperfect things.   30
And here I stand with it
Sometime in the summertime
All alone in an empty schoolroom
Where about me hang
Old maps, an abacus, pictures,
Blackboards, empty desks.
If I raise my hand
No tall teacher will demand
What I want.
But if someone in authority   40
Were here, I'd say
Give me this old world back
Whose husk I clasp
And I'll give you in exchange
The great sad real one
That's filled
Not with a child's remembered and pleasant skies
But with blood, pus, horror, death, stepmothers, and lies.

Dark Lagoon

Here lies the newborn child
Who, lately, lay within his mother
And stood beside a dark lagoon
Beneath a sunless, starless sky.
Great trees of thick foliage and stout trunks
Hid someone who, far away,
Seemed to be knocking out this epitaph
With muffled chisel on muffled stone:
"This child will someday die."
But these sounds came really   10
From his secret Sun,
His mother's heart that hung
Unseen in that dark sky.
The heart, whose tick-tocking
Was life to him, still prophesied
The ticking chisel of the monument-maker
As it should someday carve his name.
His mother's heart, the reason for his being,
Was yet the first clock he ever heard.

Here lies the baby innocent.   20
He is hardly as large
As the Gettysburg Address
And has never heard
The cry of "Eenie, meenie, minie, moe",
By which children choose a loser in a game,
And by which Fate seems to choose
Which children shall be which:
One-eyed, wilful, hare-lipped, lame,
Poor, orphans, idiots, or rich.
Nor has he read stories where   30
People cry, "I
Am betrayed"; a notion
That shall haunt him all his life
As also shall that dark lagoon
Where once he stood
And seemed in a grave
Though he had not yet been born;
And seemed to hear his mother's heart
Though also a clock
That with little clicking mouthfuls   40
Began to eat his time.

Lake Superior

I am Lake Superior
Cold and gray.
I have no superior;
All other lakes
Haven't got what it takes;
All are inferior.
I am Lake Superior
Cold and gray.
I am so cold
That because I chill them   10
The girls of Fort William
Can't swim in me.
I am so deep
That when people drown in me
Their relatives weep
For they'll never find them.
In me swims the fearsome
Great big sturgeon.
My shores are made of iron
Lined with tough, wizened trees.   20
No knife of a surgeon
Is sharper than these
Waves of mine
That glitter and shine
In the light of the Moon, my mother
In the light of the Sun, my grandmother.

Grand Bend

It is the rutting season
At Grand Bend
And the young men and the women
Explode in each other's arms
While no chaperons attend.
By this furious activity
Of the loin
No children are conceived
For they have avoided this.
While the sun   10
Sprays everyone with iodine
And old men sit
Upon the dirty beach
With great bellies big
Not with child
But with creamed asparagus.
And to somewhat more disgust
Someone has spilt a bottle of scent.
Crazily the cheap sweetness
Leaps through the air   20
Making some think of something decaying
And others of stenographers in the rain
And another to say giddily,
"How violent, at Grand Bend this year,
How violent the violets are!"

The Orphanage

We are orphans
And gleam
In our yellow dresses
(The yellow of a twenty-watt light-bulb)
Like a piece of coloured fan-light.
They lit this dingy flame
(These yellow dresses)
They that lie pasted together
In ditches by the railroad tracks
And seethe in round-shouldered cars   10
With the lusty belches of a Canadian spring.
Young men with permanent waves
Crawl over ghastly women
Whose cheeks are fat as buttocks.
Young men who play hockey
On frozen milk
And ride motorcycles
(Their horses drink the green blood of ancient ferns)
Come out to abandoned orchards
With girls   20
Who have not read Baudelaire
Or anything.

Miss Mumblecrust
Wears earrings
Like scimitars
Swinging at her ears
Swishing and cutting
Imaginary grass.
She loves
And her mouth waters   30
For the hard caramel bellies
Of young men
Who play hockey in winter.
The parts in their hair
Are like pink worms
That crawl towards us.

At night
They say
Men and women
Fit together   40
Among the elderly trees.
It is they who kindle
The yellow of our dresses.
We are the answers
To those equations
In ditches and round-shouldered cars.
And gray windows
Bob with plain white
And cretinous faces.

Klaxon

All day cars mooed and shrieked,
Hollered and bellowed and wept
Upon the road.
They slid by with bits of fur attached,
Fox-tails and rabbit-legs,
The skulls and horns of deer,
Cars with yellow spectacles
Or motorcycle monocle,
Cars whose gold eyes burnt
With a too-rich battery,   10
Murderous cars and manslaughter cars,
Chariots from whose foreheads leapt
Silver women of ardent bosom.
Ownerless, passengerless, driverless,
They came to anyone
And with headlights full of tears
Begged for a master,
For someone to drive them
For the familiar chauffeur.
Limousines covered with pink slime   20
Of children's blood
Turned into the open fields
And fell over into ditches,
The wheels kicking helplessly.
Taxis begged trees to step inside
Automobiles begged of posts
The whereabouts of their mother.
But no one wished to own them any more,
Everyone wished to walk.

The Chough

The chough, said a dictionary,
Is a relation of the raven
And a relative of the crow.
It's nearly extinct,
But lingers yet
In the forests about Oporto.
So read I as a little child
And saw a young Chough in its nest,
Its very yellow beak already tasting
The delicious eyes   10
Of missionaries and dead soldiers;
Its wicked mind already thinking
Of how it would line its frowsy nest
With the gold fillings of dead men's teeth.
When I grew older I learned
That the chough, the raven and the crow
That rise like a key signature of black sharps
In the staves and music of a scarlet sunset
Are not to be feared so much
As that carrion bird, within the brain,   20
Whose name is Devouring Years,
Who gobbles up and rends
All odds and ends
Of memory, good thoughts and recollections
That one has stored up between one's ears
And whose feet come out round either eye.

The Bird of Paradise

The bird of Paradise fades
And gray grows the Ace of Spades.
Cracked is the once loud bell
And low fall the fires of Hell.

The bird of Paradise, when wet
With dew, seemed a flying sunset;
And the Ace of Spades was blacker
Than a negro dipped in lacquer.
The bell summoned some to Heaven,
Told others it was half past eleven.   10
The fires of Hell burnt a swarm of sinners,
In their heyday, and all the winners
Of bets on horses and sweepstakes, tch!
Tch! So my tongue like the wick
Of a lamp shall someday fail
Of any glinting words and pale
Shall falter with a sigh and pout
That all Fire, all Hell, all Poetry is out.

The Tall Black Hat

As a child, I dreamt of tomorrow
Of the word "tomorrow" itself.
The word was a man in a tall black hat
Who walked in black clothes through
Green fields of quiet rain that
Beneath gray cloudfields grew.

Tall as trees or Abraham Lincoln
Were that man's brothers
Who when they become To-day
Die and dissolve one by one   10
Like licorice morning shadows
When held in the mouth of the sun.

Yesterday is an old greataunt
Rocked off in her rocking chair
To cellars where old light and snow
And all yesterdays go;
To-day was a small girl bringing
China cupfuls of water and air
And cages of robins singing,
"It is positively no crime   20

To have pleasure in Present Time."
But Tomorrow is most impressive
Like the hired man back from the fair
He comes to the child still sleeping
With pockets of longer hair,
A handful of longer fingers
And the Indian I remember
At dusk, crossing Market Square.

The man in the tall black hat
Brought the gipsy who was drunk   30
And the white faced cat
Who stepped before my stepmother
The very first time she came.

He gave the child a yellow leaf,
He holds the arrow for my heart,
He dropped the playing card in the lane,
He brought the dancing weasel,
And the old man playing the jewsharp.

He brings the wind and the sun
And the stalks of dead teazle   40
Seen on a windless winter walk,
He fetches a journey's direction
From his garden of weathervanes
And mines, like diamonds, the tears
For the glittering windowpanes
Of rain and sorrow.

All the days of all the years
The dark provider hunts me
Whom I named Sir Thomas Tomorrow
After my dream of him,   50
And in the grave fields of mystery
This black man has brothers
Who have followed him and come
Ever since with all I must see,
With Earth, Heaven and the tenor drum
I played in the C.O.T.C.,
The sound of bells and stars in a tree
Are stuck to their thumb
And lie in their tall black hats and pockets
Like pictures in locked and closed lockets.   60

At midnight he knocked and arrived
As the old woman really rocked away
And he took off his tall hat which
Changed into a small white cup,
White as the new light of day.
To the girl as small as a switch,
The girl who wakes me up,
His tallness and blackness shrank
To leave behind on the floor
From his pockets of come to pass   70
Puzzles and lonely birds to see
Diamonded names upon window glass,
A whistle, a straw and a tree.

But see out where small in the dawn
Through the hanging wingflash dance
Of the little flies, the wrens and the doves
Who are the seconds and minutes and hours
Floating over the acres of distance,
See his brother with feet of slate
Begin to walk through the wet flowers   80
Towards me with his speck of Future
And a tall black hatful of Fate.

1952

The Table of Dishes

I saw in my dream a farmer's wife
Set a table with empty dishes
On a mourning early November evening.
The light came through rain and from the stove
As she went out of the kitchen to get something.
Then it happened that the dishes talked
And did such things as you now will hear.

     * * *

Up jumped the cups, led by one old unhandled one.
Well, sang they, without us they could not get
Their tea so their mouths could be wet.   10
We have touched all their mouths; they all
Have drunk from us here, for ten miles around
At funerals and weddings: thus the cups sang,
Continuing thus while with heavier voice
Came six old worn white plates' honest cries
As they wheeled recklessly about:
Upon us do they look for their meat,
Upon us is it carefully laid down.
We, flat and smooth, hold it still for them.
We are the dish of their fatness and leanness   20
With our faithful flat old hands we shout.
Then an earthenware milk pitcher said she was sacred.
For she was the holder of white milk and life.
Then up jumped an aged soup tureen
Holloing and bellowing his giant responsibility.
The meat platter, the potato dish, the bread plate,
All sang of their happiness in service;
The knives, forks and spoons ringing bell-like
In silver quarrelings of who did most,
The whole kitchen filled with unseen, half-seen   30
Boastings, jumping up and downs of kettles, ovens,
Of lids, jars, ladles, pans, sieves and graters,
Basins, dippers, sifters, pots, dampers, lifters, pokers,
All the utensils in that darkening kitchen who
Considered their goodness, their civilization,
Their speechless, silent holding together of people,
Eating and drinking around a table.

     * * *

So they sang and danced not forgetting the grief
Of cups and dishes that break, for one broken thing
Is one less thing to carry the world's nursing nourishment,   40
One less handy cup to carry the water to the dying man's mouth,
One more step near the lapping beast's water reflection.
Up they whirled, thus singing, rejoicing, in one
Flashing earthenware white china moon shape,
Hollow, a revolving great cup made of mad dishes,
One huge grail ready for a simple lord's supper,
The oil cloth tablecloth swooping up
For the dishes its hollow to rest in,
Till the door opens and the farmer's wife
Comes up from the cellar with eggs and with meat.   50

    * * *

Oh, still table of empty set dishes, ready for six persons
To sit down and from you eat their daily bread.
Simple saucer and plain cup, holy and holder,
Quiet hands that proffer the fruits of the earth.
Oh to hold you, to hold that blessed pitcher
Whose blood, poured out,
Feeds hundreds of the poor, the lost, and thousands of the hungry,
The farmer, the toiler, the mouths old Adam's Curse
Opened in this great dish of Earth.

1953

The Horn

What is the horn that the dawn holds,
A soft shrill horn of feathers,
Cold as the dew on the grass by the paths,
Warm as the fire in the match in the box.
When this horn blows, in a sky of the sun
There rises our green star of earth
And the four evangelists who've borne
Thy bed down through the night
Now leave thee still thine eyes to see
The sun's separation of shadows.   10

Neither capons nor pullets nor hens
Can wake the sun and the world;
Only the prophets of the Old Testament
Huge old cocks, all speckled and barred,
Their wings like ragged pages of sermons,
Only they from their roosts in the henhouse
Can rouse the bread from its oven-sleep,
Raise the smoke from the haunted chimney.

Fierce old cock whose eyes look blind
So glaring and inspired are they,   20
Who live in this dungeon of cramp and dirt;
Fierce old fowl with shaking red wattles
Surrounding a beak like a kernel of wheat,
A yellow beak, plump, twisted and sharp
Which opens, hinged and prizing cry,
To show the sun's fistful of golden darts.

1953

Jordan

Clouds cross Jordan every day.
I see them disappear that way.
I press against the walls of sky,
The walls of ground and of my
Five slow senses that still meet
Only a muck beneath my feet
That's Jordan's shore but not its tide.

Who cross to the other side
Brighter than the sun become.
Trumpet, harp flute fiddle and drum   10
Do they play there in their dancing
Nearer with their psalms advancing,
Like the leaning summer earth,
Nearer the source of all their mirth.
Then they move back to rest from joy
Lest sameness delight destroy
With sounds of cloud, rain and seas
And winter winds through hollow trees.

When will my slow stars allow
Fulfillment of this longing vow?   20
I walk through holy Bible land
Blazing martyrs in my hand
Yet in learned illiteracy
Just bare letters can I see.
Yes, His spouting Dove may I get
And cannot be one drop wet.

Still I know that when not praying
Bible and candle will float by,
Water at knee and thigh not staying
But to chest and head now fly,   30
Widening eyes till they see
The golden world about that Tree
Adam saw once to disappear
Since then until recovery here.

1956

The Windyard

I built a windyard for the wind;
  The wind like a wild vast dog came up
To play with weathervanes and corners
  My keyholes and my chinks.

And for the sea I built a well;
  The brookish tomcat gurgled in,
Waterfell and sprung about
  Hunting throats and boots.

I stood a house up for the earth;
  The mappy girl came in   10
With rut and footstep path
  That wind the traveller up.

A stove I hammered for the sun;
  In flew the golden oriole
To crackle sticks of time
  And sing the leaves of space.

Come girl well yard and stove,
  Come Flesh Heart Mind and Lyre,
Come Earth Water Wind and Fire.   20
      Well, when they came
Barking, meowing, talking and caroling,
I stepped above both house and yard
      Into myself.

1956

Writing and Loving

Grammar's mistake is Love's correctness:
She likes the fused sentence, the commafault kiss,
Abhors loving the interior of one's clothes, the period,
The colon, the semicolon . . . bars to conjunction.

The periodic sentence definites the usually indefinite
Article; the paratactic she-sentence, with her verb
At the beginning & 1000's of modifiers after,
Spreads wide her subordinate clauses & colours
His infinitive with her introductory modifier
Until after some careful parallelism,   10
Slowly breaking into phrases, words mere
Letters of the alphabet until a blank page of ecstasy.

1956

44

The Sparrow

His feathers are the dark subway
Dripping with train oil and rain
His voice is the funny squeak chalk
That draws the obscene twain
Ogre and ogress eight feet long:
Sing their wedding, ding dung
        Ding dung chirp chirp
Underneath the timely thunder of the trains.

Beneath the level of the street
In a grotto of frozen stale urine   10
Stand the gods of stolen chalk
Scoured by the tunnel wind;
Trains and cars and feet and bicycles
Dance above the waiting festering dolls:
Sing sparrows at their wedding
        Ding dung, cheep cheep cheep cheep
The old newspapers fly up like jangled brains.

Speculation seizes on the possibility
Of lights flaring wherever these are worshipped.
How many times here? Once for a certainty   20
In the episcopal garage; hark, the city's glowing—
An intense white light for animals, blue for
Paederasts, purple for nocturnal effusions, for
Onan a green light and yellow for the normal.
        Hymen Sparrow, bring the torches:
Clatter clatter clatter clatter
        Chirp chirp ding dung bell
I walked through the city lit by love.

Dirty, diseased, impish, unsettling, rapist
Illegitimate, urban, southless, itching,   *30*
Satyromaniac, of butcher string the harpist,
The sparrows and their gods are everything.
I like to hear their lack of tune
On a very cold winter snowy afternoon.
They must be listened to and worshipped each—
The shocking deities: ding dung is sacred
      So is filthiness, obscenity
            Chirp, chirp.
Even whores can on occasion muster up a grail.

Christ and Gautama and Emily Bronte were   *40*
Born in the midst of angelic whir
In a dripping concrete den under,
Under the alimentary trains: it is we
Who see the angels as brown lechery
And the sacred pair—Venus and Adonis
As automatons coupled as a train is.
      And so step down my chalky reader,
            Why keep our festival here
                  In this crotch?
            Ding dung chirp chirp: *50*
A sparrow sings if you but have an ear.

1958

The Hummingbird

The hum of an approaching christening mob!
The hanging still in the air with so much motion
He flies with wings of air in an air of feathers!
The hanging still in the air with so much motion

The hollow twig that transports flowers to his blood
The barn of flowers pressed in a jumping ounce
No song is needed when one is a song
The barn of flowers pressed in a jumping ounce

Enoch, Elijah or Ascension is your name
My dainty jaunt, why call I you these names?   *10*
Because I realize and advertise that there
Far down the dark row of mountains cowering
That ruby flash that is the chariot of fire
            Is your throat too.

1958

Doomsday, or the Red Headed Woodpecker

I

    Red Sky!
    Morning!
Shaking like a scarlet head!
    Doomsday!
    Rise up!
Spring your lids, you dead!
    Scrape out
    Coffins!
Put yourself together!
    Pat that dust!   10
    Find that bust!
This is the last weather!
    Trumpet!
    Drummer!
    Thunder!
Vomit you cannibals!
    Shake out those
    Those old flesh dresses
For the resurrection parties and balls!

II

Here comes St. Sebastian with a handful of arrows!   20
  The big threshing woodpecker is
  Beating on the green drum!
Here comes the poor boy who got caught in the harrows!
Here comes St. Bartholomew with his skin!
        Scroll away!
        Hell this way!
        Heaven that!
        Rat a tat tat!
There goes Death and there goes Sin!
  Here come Cain and Abel   30
        Hand in hand!
Here come horizontals pursued by slopes,
        Here comes a table
    Changing back to a tree and
Here come the hanged people skipping with their ropes!

III
    Red Sky!
    Morning!
Shaking like a scarlet head!
    Doomsday!
    Rise up!   40
Spring your lids, you dead!
    Scrape out
    Coffins!
Put yourself together!
    Pat that dust!
    Find that bust!
This is the last weather!
    Trumpet!
    Drummer!
    Thunder!   50
Vomit you cannibals!
    Shake out those
    Those old flesh dresses
For the resurrection parties and balls!

1958

The Executioner of Mary Stuart

There was a jolly headsman once
Attached to an ancient castle.
They chose him specially for his task—
    To murder other rascals.

For example I have often felt
My analogy might be
A rat-trap made from the bones of rats
    And that was simple old me.

So my life was ruined but I
Was given a sort of reward: 10
The clothes of the executed,
    Often some astonishing rich brocade.

One day I caught in my jaws
A woman who dazzled the sun.
I chopped off her head as my task
    And took what was left for my fun.

Annunciation to the Mud
In the beginning was the Dark
Bridegroom to a headless Queen,
    Far off I hear the hell dogs bark.   20

1958

The Morning Dew

Shake seed of light and thunder
From where you hang,
The Word without the Flesh.

The pastures, sloughs and trees all shine
Their leaves and grasses sown
With flashing tears.

Here is Absalom's hair in crystal terms
Feverish bonfire of the sensual body,
Bloodbob.

Sharp, sharp yellow teeth, sharp sharp   10
In the dark mouth blinking of the
Fox-haired queen.

Blue as the fields of flax in the summer
That dream of retting, spreading, drying,
White linen snow.

Green as the thoughtful ancient woods
Ash contemplation of linden tree thinking,
Paththrough.

The killdeer's nest is built of gold,
Cobwebs are blessed and Eden   20
Has caught these fields within her fold.

1958

The Yellow-Bellied Sapsucker

I

The terrifying form of the pebble,
The awful hieroglyph of the dewdrop,
The obscure character of the ravelled string,
The mysterious letter of the bent straw,
The teeming message of the dead groundhog,
The difficult sentence of the old beggar with two canes,
And the whore on Yonge Street with her stockings rolled down,
    Such a suffix hard to render:
The untranslatable participles of the rushing wind,
The gentle telegram in a dank code from the firefly swamp,   10
    The golden feather on the path through the bush
        That flew a song in a lost language.

II

    The pebble towered dark and purple over me,
    The dewdrop made me doubt my value,
    The ravelled string hanged me with despair,
    There was no lexicon for the straw letter,
    The groundhog's sea of worms sickened,
The two caned sentence disappeared down the road,
The short runty cabbie on his night off picked her up,
The dead leaves, the lightning, the thunder and the rainbow   20
    Sailed away with the wind but I didn't,
    The blinking swamp led me muddy nowhere,
And the feather, it was just a feather, nothing but.

III

Came Christ the Tiger and Buddha the Balloon
Hercules the Lion and Bacchus the Drunkard
Emily the Prostitute of Snow, and Dan Trot
Sly Tod, Reverend Jones, Kitty Cradle
Baby Cobbler with his Rattle Sparkle
Mad William Lyon with his bastard and Blake
With his trained angels, Spenser with his   30
Creepyland, Shakespeare with his no-handed Lavinia,
St. John with the Seven Days wound up,
Nothing left but miles of Sabbath,
Solomon who sang of his foot in the doorway,
Gorgeous salesman, Sterne with his
Involved snigger: came Love, Innocence,
Rainbow, Whirlwind and Falling Star.

IV
                    And then
The pebble was a mountain that took years to climb
The dewdrop was all reality itself   40
The string was the pathway to Heaven
The straw formed God's name
The groundhog meant that Death was laughter
The old beggar with the sack on his back
Was God the Father bearing up his creation
With Adam and Eve the two canes before him,
To what journey's end? perhaps some hayloft
With the rain beating down on the owly roof.
The Whore was the Holy Ghost herself,
"The dearling noursling of his bosome," Sophia,   50
Who told him how to make it all "at her behest."
        The wind was the world of words, all poetry
        At its giant blind Pentecostal source,
The nine mused and pleated winnowing fan of wisdom,
The fireflies led me to Noah's Ark,
        And the golden feather sang:

V

                Existence has a yellow belly
                        And sucks sap
                It pecks life in a dead tree.
                It is a boyish drummer   60

                Who takes the stick of life
                        So powerful
                And takes that fork's wife
                So wise, the spoon of death

                And beats out upon the drum
                Of the third state, the other room
                Rented to both right and wrong
                To both death and life . . . Eternity!

                Eternity, that drum, sang the bird.
                Play on it with life and with death!   70

VI
> The scene changes:
> The mountain is a pebble in your hand
> The abyss of Space is a dewdrop
> > Heaven Road lies ravelled in your pocket
> > Time's cloud of moments is a rain drop
> > > On the fence,
> > God lies even in our excrement
> > What Bible says, a groundhog babbles too,
> > > A passerby is the Creator
> The holy Ghost is your wife or husband,   80
> > Shakespeare, your whistle,
> And the thousand eyes of fancy make each idle stare
> > Possible breakthrough to the perfect.

VII
> > Golden Feather
> > Of the yellow bellied sapsucker
> > You are a golden spring
> > . A golden voice
> > A golden tree and a golden torch
> By whose light and in whose world
> I show all complexity unfurled.   90

1959

52

Rachel

I
When I was a young man
    Passing the city dump
In the smoking rubbish I heard
    A small and rusty wail.

    Naked
    Unwashed from the caul
    Thy navel string uncut
A crusted, besmattered and loathsome thing.

I fouled my clothes and stank
    But I brought you to my house.   10
I found that your mother was a gypsy,
    Your father an Indian.

But "Live!" I said, and you lived.
    You grew like a field of flax,
Your hair was gold as the sun,
    Your breasts were blossoms.

I walked by your foster house,
    It was the time of love.
I rewarded your governess for
    Pearly runs in your Scarlatti.   20

II
It was the time of love
I was so afraid you'd say no
My heart beat like giant footsteps
I felt agony in your garden.

    Again you came to my house,
I was ashamed to ask you so often,
    I gave you a golden ring
        And a glass pen.

    You dressed in silk
    You bathed in milk   30
    But as we embraced
On your shoulder I saw the red speck.

    Never had it washed off.
    Yet with all the more love
        I went unto you
And you prospered into a kingdom.

III
I must go away to abroad.
When I returned uptown
I met you and you knew me not,
Your hair like flax tow   40

Crimped like an eggbeater, your
Mouth like a cannibal's—bloody,
Your eyelids massive with blue mud,
A handmuff of bats fur.

I found out your carryings on,
Your lovers and infidelities.
You sold my child to a brothel,
You had to pay for your men.

In pity, I bribed men to go to you,
To your two biggest lovers,   50
Lord Dragon and Count Ceros,
I whispered your infamies.

They gathered their mobs of devils,
In the name of virtue they attacked
Your tall town house
As you bore a seven month bastard.

Out on your balcony they brought you,
Your house devoured with fire.
Out they threw you and the dogs
Licked your blood up.   60

IV
Then from your hand I took
My ring, from the witch's hand
I took my golden ring.
Her breast was a dungheap.

Her child I found and I
Washed you in my tears.
Still on your shoulder is the
Red speck that I know.

I wash you with my tears
And still the speck remains.   70
It is my fault, my darling,
That I have not tears enough.

1959

Granny Crack

I was a leather skinned harridan
I wandered the county's roads
Trading and begging and fighting
With the sun for hat and the road for shoes.

You played a pigsty Venus
When you were young, old dame,
In the graveyard or behind the tavern.
The burdock girl was your name.

She talked vilely it is remembered,
Was a moving and walking dictionary   10
Of slang and unconventional language
The detail of her insults was extraordinary.

We dozen scoundrels laid you
For a quarter each in the ditch
To each you gave the sensation
That we were the exploited bitch.

You saw me freckled and spotted
My face like a killdeer's egg
When, berry-picking kids, you ran from me
Frightened down the lane by the wood.   20

They saw her as an incredible crone
The spirit of neglected fence corners,
Of the curious wisdom of brambles
And weeds, of ruts, of stumps and of things despised.

I was the mother of your sun
I was the sister of your moon
My veins are your paths and roads
On my head I bear steeples and turrets
I am the darling of your god.

1959

The Ghost

The evening waddles over the fields like a turkey.
I lurk,
Where my knowledge was chopped from my power.
All knowledge waits for you at the corner here so murky.

The awkward doltish low I.Q. farmboy shambles down the steps,
The empty echoing pitcher in his hand:
I am!
Ha ha! And his hair stands straight up like brambles.

Everything — Egyptian hieroglyphs and crystallography,
Diary of shadows,   10
Vast God and the interiors of tree trunks, snowflakes
All spin like a fiery corkscrew into his psychology.

For I know everything now having passed into source,
Even
Through me he knows himself — a kidnapped prince.
It is too much for him — he falls down — hoarse
As they shriek and lift him up — I am not.

The evening waddles over the fields like a turkey.
I lurk,
Where my knowledge was severed from my power.   20
All knowledge waits for you at the corner here so murky.

1959

From A SEQUENCE IN FOUR KEYS

i) The Dwarf

Six inches of my six foot pa
Compressed my height to these three feet.
On Sabbath day he sold me to
The castle of the starry street

There I sleep in a cradle and amuse
The castle with my minority.
No, I am not someone far away.
Reach out and touch me.

I plucked a berry for the young queen
Such fruit as drove her mad.   10
She haunts the stables and the mews,
Is serviced by the coachman's lad.

I stole the tall crown prince's toy
And put it in his brother's chest.
He knocked his brother out of life
With father's curse he fled to east.

The servants swore that they saw angels;
I said that they must grovel,
I sneered and laughed at all their visions.
Now they see only hovel.   20

The swineherd was a noble man,
More noble than my lord.
With a whicker-whack I tripped him up.
His brow now levels swineward.

'Twas I who hid beneath the bed
When the princess planned elopement.
They got as far as the Scarlet Sea
When my lord's riders they met.

I filled their hearts with maddening lust,
I made three eyes unfashionable,   30
I filled their hearts with maddening chastity,
I split them into sexual.

Lady Air and Sir Earth,
Alderman Water and the Earl of Fire,
Yeoman Quintessence and Miss Light
I set at jar and gyre and ire.

From this casement look ye out
At rotting sheep and mildewed crop.
There's the minstrel limping off
I bade them yesterday his tongue lop.   40

The castle's empty, wonder none —
I bade them re-build it inside out.
Their fire flew up into the sun,
Their cistern rolled into a moon.

In a great battle my dear lord
Killed and was killed by the crown prince.
I've holed up here among the ruins
The compressed cause of everything.

The only thing I know how to do
Is crawl into this manger.   50
I'll prop the dead queen's body up,
Perhaps 'twill fool a stranger.

Come here shepherds.   Here's the way.
Bah bah bah for an incarnation.
This way aristocratic intelligence.
Meow meow for a new sensation!

To the curious observant baby
The humble and the royal bow.
Hush a bye my baby do, for see —
The spider on your mother's brow.   60

ii) The Baby

Small babe, tell me
        As you sat in your mother's cave
What did you build there,
        Little baby mine?

Sir, I made the tooth
        I invented the eye
I played out hair on a comb-harp
        I thought up the sigh.

I pounded the darkness to
        Guts, Heart and Head: 10
America, Eurasia and Africa
        I out of chaos led.

I fought the goblins
        For the heart;
'Twas a jewel they desired,
        But I held it.

I fought off the rats
        From the guts
They nibbled but I
        Smashed the mutts.   20

I choked the bat so intent
        For the diamond of my mind;
I caught him in the ogre's cellar
        The tub of blood behind.

And the darkness gave me
        Two boneless wands or swords;
I knew not their meaning then
        Whether traps or rewards.

One was the vorpal phallus
        Filled with jostling army,   30
Henhouse and palace
        Street crowds and history.

Two was the magic tongue
        Stuffed with names and numbers,
The string of song
        The waker from fallen slumbers.

My mother opened her grave
        I sprang out a giant
Into another cave
        Where I was a seed again,   40

Helpless and wriggly small
        As in my father's groin;
My Shakespeare's tongue a wawl
        And impotent my loin.

The sun-egg I must reach
        Was steeples far away,
The world that I must name
        Was shapeless, sneaky gray.

Is it wonder then I rage
        An old man one hour old,   50
A bridegroom come to a bride
        Careless unready and cold.

My wedding cake's still in the field;
        My bride is ninety and maggotty;
My groomsmen glaring hangmen;
        My bridal bed bouldery.

Small babe, tell me
        As you sit in your mother's cave
What do you build there,
        Little baby mine?   60

iv) The Lost Child

Long have I looked for my lost child.
I hear him shake his rattle
Slyly in the winter wind
In the ditch that's filled with snow.

He pinched and shrieked and ran away
At the edge of the November forest.
The hungry old burdock stood
By the dead dry ferns.

Hear him thud that ball!
The acorns fall by the fence.   10
See him loll in the St. Lucy sun,
The abandoned sheaf in the wire.

Oh Life in Death! my bonny nursling
Merry drummer in the nut brown coffin,
With vast wings outspread I float
Looking and looking over the empty sea

And there! in the — on the rolling death
Rattling a dried out gourd
Floated the mysterious cradle
Filled with a source.   20

I push the shore and kingdom to you,
Oh winter walk with seedpod ditch:
I touch them to the floating child
And lo! Cities and gardens, shepherds and smiths.

1959

The Man Hunter

After the flare of the illegal action
"A Mr. Ledger was found murdered"
Society assembles me, fills my heart
With blood, my brain with purpose and my

I walk through the arranged spaces
Plain clothes over my iron flesh:
I go to alleys, lanes, squares & places,
I tip the beer parlour this way & that.

I pull the transom to me
And walk through baby's minds   10
I climb through the children's game
And negotiate the hopscotch rinds.

Bye bye Baby Bunting
Daddy's gone a-hunting
Gone to get a criminal's skin
To wrap my Baby Bunting in.

I am caught in the old woman's hair;
That pumpkin she calls her head
Cannot remember; the brick leaves flutter,
The steel trees and the cement underwood.   20

I have reached the turn in the path,
The ford through the fountains of traffic,
I hang on a saliva rope from the tramp's
Cliff-face—it is the last mountain.

The pawn ticket: Mr. Ledger's obscene music box.
Existence fastens its minute teeth in my
The advertising hits with its whore-sonnets
The street car crawls up my thigh

The chestnut leaves play card games,
The street lights each have a separate system of shadows,   30
I come to my Sleeping Beauty, my New Jerusalem,
The man with the words on his forehead: FORGIVE ME

Front Street and Duke Street and Jarvis
I married my hempen princess
Timothy Eaton Memorial United Church
I put a human neck in her circle.

1959

From A MESSAGE TO WINNIPEG

ii) Winnipeg Seen as a Body of Time and Space

Winnipeg, what once were you. You were,
Your hair was grass by the river ten feet tall,
Your arms were burr oaks and ash leaf maples,
Your backbone was a crooked silver muddy river,
Your thoughts were ravens in flocks, your bones were   50
     snow,
Your legs were trails and your blood was a people
     Who did what the stars did and the sun.

Then what were you? You were cracked enamel like
Into parishes and strips that come down to the river.
Convents were built, the river lined with nuns
Praying and windmills turning and your people
Had a blood that did what a star did and a Son.

Then on top of you fell
A boneyard wrecked auto gent, his hair   60
Made of rusted car door handles, his fingernails
Of red Snowflake Pastry signs, his belly
Of buildings downtown; his arms of sewers,
His nerves electric wires, his mouth a telephone,
His backbone—a cracked cement street. His heart
An orange pendulum bus crawling with the human fleas
Of a so-so civilization—half gadget, half flesh—
     I don't know what I would have instead—
    And they did what they did more or less.

iii) Le Tombeau de Pierre Falcon

Pierre Falcon,
You say here along with this unsingable music
That on June nineteenth these Burnt Wood people
Ah yes, the Métis were dark, so called Bois-Brûlés,
Arrived near this settlement of Lord Selkirk's
Fort Douglas

You say in this second verse that your Burnt Woods
Took three foreigners prisoner at Frog Plain.   80
These foreigners were Scotchmen from the Orkneys
Who had come, as you put it, to rob your—Pierre
    Falcon's—
Country.

Well we were just about to unhorse
When we heard two of us give, give voice.
Two of our men cried, "Hey! Look back, look back!
    The Anglo-Sack
    Coming for to attack."

Right away smartly we veered about
Galloping at them with a shout!   90
You know we did trap all, all those Grenadiers!
    They could not move
    Those horseless cavaliers.

Now we like honourable men did act,
Sent an ambassador—yes, in fact!
"Monsieur Governor! Would you like to stay?
    A moment spare—
    There's something we'd like to say."

Governor, Governor, full of ire.
"Soldiers!" he cries, "Fire! Fire."   100
So they fire the first and their muskets roar!
    They almost kill
    Our ambassador!

Governor thought himself a king.
He wished an iron rod to swing.
Like a lofty lord he tries to act.
    Bad luck, old chap!
    A bit too hard you whacked!

When we went galloping, galloping by
Governor thought that he would try   110
For to chase and frighten us Bois-Brûlés.
    Catastrophe!
    Dead on the ground he lay.

Dead on the ground lots of grenadiers too.
Plenty of grenadiers, a whole slew.
We've almost stamped out his whole army.
    Of so many
    Five or four left there be.

You should have seen those Englishmen—
Bois-Brûlés chasing them, chasing them.   120
From bluff to bluff they stumbled that day
    While the Bois-Brûlés
    Shouted "Hurray!"

And now in this eleventh verse you ask
Who made up this song and then you tell us
That you yourself made it up—Pierre Falcon.
You made it up to sing the glory of the
Burnt Wood People.

Far away and dear, spunky old and early poet
I wish I could sing the praises of the Neon People   130
To You.

vi) Winnipeg as a Chess Game

It is a game of chess or checkers.
No, it is a game of chess
For we have not all the same
Income, outcome, stations, riches.
It is a game of civilization
Played on squares of Night and Day.
A life in a city, a life in playing
Games of getting up and going to bed,
Being alive and being so dead,
How to be good and how to be bad   190
Upon the squares of summer,
In the corner of spring
With the children skipping,
In the white streets of winter
Beneath the brown leaves with trees on them
In the fall park.

I went
Down the streets where I have seen
In an upstairs room, the White Queen,
With a bicycle beside her bed.   200
I looked
In a window on York Street,
Saw the White Knight and three pawns
All round a table eating their supper.
I had not had mine yet and loved
The match girl orphan loneliness
Of watching other people eating theirs:
Passing the saltshaker, reaching for the butter.
The rest of the white pawns rushed through the street,
Playing games of frontier and boycows and buffalogirls;   210
They skipped with pieces of string coming
With secretive paper bags out of the Gem Store.

Everytime I go out I bring back
A face I love, a face I didn't notice,
I bring back another black piece,
Another white one for the game.
I met the black pieces on Donald Street.
Beside the funeral home I saw a yellow car.
Then in the night they come toward me
Dark, dark faces, negroes in ones and twos   220
Going towards the funeral of their black king,
King of the black people in a city of snow.

Down this street I went and saw
A small girl shooting with a bow and arrow.
Her father's house was a house where
Hands and cups were read and she
Was a pawn in the centre of the board.

Down the street the streetcar comes
And while it comes you cannot talk   230
Until you board it, the old streetcar
Young once in Philadelphia sixty years ago they say,
Long room with a stove, company,
Strangers and green moss to sit upon.
As we move to see the Black Queen,
The White Bishop, old Canon Bastion,
Is on the car with us and says Hello.
He never understands but has a voice
Fit for anything in the King James Version

We go to see the Black Queen   240

Each day after Christmas the sun sets farther north
Of Broadway

All these white streets of winter
Filled with walking people
This castle turns a corner
This woman takes a pawn
Reader I present you with a chessboard in the snow

1960

The Alphabet

Where are the fields of dew?
I cannot keep them.
They quip and pun
The rising sun
Who plucks them out of view:
But lay down fire-veined jasper!

For out of my cloudy head
Come Ay Ee I Oh and U,
Five thunders shouted;
Drive in sardonyx!   10

And Ull Mm Nn Rr and hisSsings
Proclaim huge wings;
Pour in sea blue sapphires!

Through my bristling hair
Blows Wuh and Yuh
Puh, Buh, Phuh and Vuh,
The humorous air:
Lift up skies of chalcedony!

Huh, Cuh, Guh and Chuh
Grunt like pigs in my acorn mind: 20
Arrange these emeralds in a meadow!

Come down Tuh, Duh and Thuh!
Consonantly rain
On the windowpane
Of the shrunken house of the heart;
Lift up blood red sardius!

Lift up golden chrysolite!
Juh, Quuh, Zuh and X
Scribble heavens with light,
Steeples take fright.   30

In my mouth like bread
Stands the shape of this glory;
Consonants and vowels
Repeat the story:
And sea-green beryl is carried up!

The candle tongue in my dark mouth
Is anguished with its sloth
And stung with self-scoff
As my eyes behold this treasure.
Let them bring up topaz now!   40

Dazzling chrysoprase!
Dewdrops tempt dark wick to sparkle.
Growl Spark! you whelp and cur,
Leap out of tongue kennel
And candle sepulchre.

I faint in the hyacinthine quarries!
My words pursue
Through the forest of time
The fading antlers of this dew.

A B C D E F G H I J K L M   50
Take captive the sun
Slay the dew quarry
Adam's Eve is morning rib
Bride and bridegroom marry
Still coffin is rocking crib
Tower and well are one
The stone is the wind, the wind is the stone
New Jerusalem
N O P Q R S T U V W X Y Z !

1960

67

The Butterfly and the Moth

The Earth, that huge & dirty Lout,
Has my five bonfires all put out.
See these two pebbles, they're my eyes,
My ears have changed to windy skies,
My tongue's become a dead snail shell
And brown leaves paste my sense of smell.
My instruments of pleasure are
The dead weeds' winter wind guitar.
With rotten sighs and whizzing sounds
I fade in a thousand burial grounds.

Alas, beneath the drifts of snow
No greens for caterpillars grow.
I'll build of nothing and of sorrow
From ashes and of autumn dust
A cradle coffin ark which must
Somehow float me to tomorrow.

In my dead hands grows a fine grass,
The waste fork sprouts a mushroom.
In my eyes come the Sun & the Moon;
I hear again the South Wind pass,
In my nails rise rain white clouds.
My empty head teems flower crowds,
And sing me to a Butterfly
Who wise & reckless passes by
The tight closed flowers of death and doth
Leave them for the brown winged moth.

1961

To Bishop Berkeley

How beautiful the barnyard is,
    The little flashlight says.
Wherever I look is shining
    And active as plays.

So says the lamp within the house
    At golden plaster, golden walls
And candles remark how wainscot
    Gleams like calls.

Even the urinal match said,
    Oh what beautiful hands,   10
And the oozy willow-the-wisp
    Marvelled blue quicksands.

Oh Wordsworth and nature-walkers
    Thy nature barnyard is;
Her trees are plaster, wainscot hills,
    Handy vale and miry mess.

Wherever walks your lantern self
    The crop of wonder then sprouts up;
        Five kinds of music,
The spear of time, the spatial cup.   20

1961

Near Tobermory, Ontario

I look upon a blue cove
    In August
With egg pebble beach,
Blue sky & cedar birch sides.

And I look upon the sisters four
    Blue sky & blue water
    Rock, pebble & earth
And the light I see it with.

Watty Blue has a drowned man
    For her heart   10
And rain for food & wind
To crisp her thoughts with.

Pale Blue Airy has clouds
To mind & winds to sing,
Thunder to say, lightning to do
    And birds to hold.

Urtha lumpily clogs
    Her clotty feet,
Waves Aaron's Rod & wears
    Emeralds in rags.   20

But Light, you're quite another thing.
    Indeterminate,
You hold them all yet let them slip
    Into themselves again.

1963

Starling with a Split Tongue

Some boys caught me
    In the yard
And with a jackknife they
Split my tongue into speech
So in a phrenological cage
Here in the garage I stay
    And say
The cracklewords passersby taught.
I say I know not what
Though I pray I do not pray   10
Though I curse I do not curse
Though I talk I do not talk

"I thought that made it kinda nice"
I heard her say as she began slipping on the ice
    The the I am   An a am I
    I and am are the & a   Who is are? Who saw war?
I rock a little pronoun   It does instead of me
I rose as I   Nooned as you
Lay down as he or she   Begat we, you & they
My eggs are covered with commas   20

    "Yuh remember when she fell down in a fit?"
    Reveries Jake from the bottom of the pit.

Before beforeday   after St. After's Massacre
While the while is on   Since since is since
Let's wait till till   Or until if you like
I come from from   to Whither Bay
Down Whence Road   but not To-day

As still as infinitives were the   Stones
Filled with adjectives were the   Trees
And with adverbs the   Pond   30
This all is a recorded announcement
              This all is a recorded announcement
"I thought that made it kinda nice"
"Yuh remember . . . . in a fit?"
                   Darkness deep
Now fills the garage and its town
              With wordless sleep.

Who split their tongues? I ask.
Of Giant Jackknife in the sky.
Who split their tongues into lie mask   40
And lie face; split their hand
Into this way, that way, up and down,
Divided their love into restless hemispheres,
Split into two — one seeing left, one right
Their once one Aldebaran all-seeing eye?
In the larger garage of the endless starlight
        Do they not croak as I?

1964

From   THE YOUNG TRAVELLER

i) Going for the Mail

After four, when home from school
    A boy down the farm walks,
To get the mail the mailman's left
    In the backroad mailbox.

Oh things to watch and things to think
    As I walk down the lane
Between the elmtree and the fence
    Things that are not plain.

For instance is the elmtree there
    Still there when I am past it?   10
I jump about and there it is
    Certain to all my wit.

But could it still not be
    That when my back is turned
It disappears and nothing is?
    Why not, I've still not learned.

There's sedge in the marsh to look at
    And dark brown curled dock.
Why do I love the weeds so
    And examine every stalk?   20

Back at the house they tell him
    That although he was at the mailbox
He forgot to get the mail out
    So back again he walks.

The fields are dark, the sky dark gray
    The farmhouse lights come on
And dimmer lights in barns,
    One reflected in the pond.

This time there's less to think upon
    Since all the detail's gone   30
But what news and what mail I get
    To reflect upon –

The world in huge butterflies of paper –
    (And here's the comfort)
Will still not be as interesting
    As walking twice for it.

iv) The Stoneboat

What is a stoneboat you want to know?
    A stoneboat is a wooden sleigh
That bumping glides over grass or loam
    And does not need the snow.

In that plowed field over there
    We're told to pick up the stones.
To the stoneboat lying in the yard
    We hitch up the blind mare.

From its weed entangled rest
    She lurches out the stoneboat   10
From underneath a mouse streaks out
    And we see its brown grass nest.

In the nest are little pink things
    At least a dozen of them,
A blind soft rose in the dry brown nest
    Of faint movings and squeakings.

On no wheels, on only itself
    The wooden boat glides on.
Down the cowpath lane stream
    Like a square wooden swan.   20

To the brown ocean field where float
    The mysterious scattered stones:
Pink, blue, speckled and gray
    We tote them onto the stone boat.

What are you, speckled egg-shaped stone?
    You cannot speak, you cannot see
    You cannot hear, but can you think?
For you seem blessed with a life of your own.

In the gray sky fades the sun.
    We turn back to the yard   30
With a cargo of stones each different
    We unhitch and our job is done.

Their mother has carried the pink mice away.
    The blind mare eats her supper grass.
The blind stones dream on the curious ship
    And the blind world waits for the day.

1964

A :
ᵦ V ᴧ A;
'TSCI ꓱ H:
;EBAᵷI ᗡIꟼ ;
ꜱ u EₓV ꬵᴛ :
'DT TUVMℤₑ7   ꜱ
ꜱ Qₐₑꜱ ꜱ   ꟼLⱵⱭꟻESV ꜱ
no oooooₒₒₒₒₒMWTℤ ꜱ . Ɐ ꜱ Ν ℳⱭᵤₒ ooooo ou
ᵌᵥq   o o ooo   ꜱ ꞁ ꞁ .   Ʌᵥ o ꞁ
ꞁ   o   o   ᵥ ꞁꞁ ꞁꞁꞁ ꞁ   ꞁ ꞁⱼₓ   o   ꞁ
ꞁₐ ᵥ ᴢᵤᵤ ᵥᵥ Xᵣ ꞁꞁ ꞁꞁ,ₛ ꞁꞁꞁ ꞁꞁꞁ   ᵣXₘₘ ꭍd'',ₛₘ ꞁ
ꞁꞁꞁꞁꞁꞁ ꞁꞁꞁꞁꞁᵣꞁꞁꞁꞁꞁꞁꞁꞁꞁꞁꞁꞁ ꞁꞁꞁ ꞁꞁ ᵣꞁ ꞁ O ꞁꞁꞁꞁꞁꞁꞁꞁꞁꞁꞁ ꞁꞁ.ₐ.ꞁꞁꞁꞁꞁꞁꞁ ꞁꞁꞁꞁꞁꞁ
ꞅꞅꞅ ꞅ ᵣꞅ ꞅₒ ꞅ ꞅꞅ ꞅꞅꞅ,''',''' ꞁꞁꞁ Ⱶꞁꞁꞁꞁᵤᵥ''',' ꞅ ꞅ ꞅ ꞅ ꞅ ꜱ ... ꭍꞁꞁ
ₑ ꜱꜱꜱꜱꜱꜱꜱꜱꜱꜱꜱꜱ ꜱ ꜱꜱꜱₐₛ·ꜱꜱꜱꜱꜱꜱꜱꜱꜱ.: ꞮHꟻⱭꜱꜱꜱₐꜱꜱꜱꜱꜱꜱꜱꜱꜱꜱꜱꜱꜱꜱꜱꜱꜱꜱꜱꜱꜱꜱꜱꜱ ꜱꜱ
ₑ A Xꜱ ᴨ Ɫ ꜱꜱ ꜱ ꜱₓꜱₒ ꞁₑ G   ₑ . ꜱ ᵤ ₓ ꜱ ₑꞁ ꞁz ᵌꜱℯ ℯ
ₑ ꭍ ꜱ₉ꭍ A ꜱꜱ   ꜱ ᵦ Ν   ℯ ꞁꞁ ꞁ   ℤ ꜱ ꞁ d ₉ ●
ℯ ᴣ ℯᴦ Đ   ℯ   ☰   ℯ   ℯ ꞓ ᴄᵤᵥ
●DEO D   ꞓ   Ӽ   ℯ   SUTTANᴘₑ
ꜱ ꝺᵤᵌꞁ ꜱ   O   ꜱ   ᵥₐ ꞁᵤₓƷ
ꞁ. ᵣ ꞁ ꞁ   ꞁꞁ   ꞁ   ꞁꞁ
Ꞽ₂₂₂ꞮHꞁꞢꞢƳ   ꞁ   KꞱꞀꞀℤꞀꞀꞌƳ
NꞀꞀꞀꞀꞀꞀꞀN   !!!   ᴡᴡᴡᴧꞰᴍ
ICHꟼꞘꞒꞘHꞒꞒ   GHHꞒꞒꞘꞒꞓꞮ
ꭍꭍꭍꭍꭍ   ꭍꭍꭍꭍꭍꭍꭍ ꭍᵤꞁ
ꞏꞏꞏꞏ   ꭍ

The Butterfly

From Time's cocoon
And the caterpillar of prophecy
Comes to Bethlehem
A shining laughing baby butterfly.

This butterfly is Christ whom we
Since He is the Word made flesh
Do fashion verbally.

1961

75

Gifts

Existence gives to me
What does he give to thee?

He gives to me :	a pebble
He gives to me :	a dewdrop
He gives to me :	a piece of string
He gives to me :	a straw

Pebble   dewdrop   piece of string   straw

The pebble is a huge dark hill I must climb
The dewdrop's a great storm lake you must cross
The string was a road he could not find   10
The straw will be a sign whose meaning they forget

Hill   lake   road   sign

What was it that quite changed the scene
So desert fades into meadows green?

The answer is that they met a Tiger
The answer is that he met a Balloon,
A Prostitute of Snow, a Gorgeous Salesman
As well as a company of others such as
Sly Tod, Reverend Jones, Kitty Cradle and so on

Who was the Tiger?   Christ   20
Who was the Balloon?   Buddha
Emily Brontë and the Emperor Solomon
Who sang of his foot in the doorway.
All these met him. They were hopeful and faithful.

Now the mountain becomes   a pebble in my hand
The lake calms down   to a dewdrop in a flower
The weary road   is a string around your wrist
The mysterious sign   is a straw that whistles "Home"

Pebble   dewdrop   piece of string   straw

1965

The Killdeer

There was nothing left but the killdeer.
   He skated the cold spring air
Over the old pasture, the line of elms,
   The Easter farmhouse, I there

     Heard him cry:
There lived a man by Spiral Lake
   And he my grandfather was;
Seven children did he make
   And this is what their names were:

Mars and Mercury were two little boys,   *10*
   Luna and Venus the girls:
Jupiter and Saturn had moons for toys
   And their brother Sun for light, sir.

In my grandfather's spacious garden groin
   His tree of children grew,
And grandchild I in my earthy nest
   There first sung and flew.

I went to school with Milky Way;
   She was the daughter of Spiral Lake,
Oh little Milky, temporal and speckled,   *20*
   Cow-pocked, milk-splashed and gay.

But the farm-nest tipped
   And Father split in two;
Uncle Good and Aunt Evil
   Took me in, how do you do.

They lived in a House of Day
   It had a Yard of Night;
It stood on a street of Puzzle Town
   On a refuse graveyard site.

Behind the gasworks Cain got me.   *30*
   He crushed me like a nettle.
A sweet faced boy named Abel brought me
   His dearest treasure, a piece of gravel.

After he died his brother Seth
   Spat out the apple-pip
And said with magic breath;
   Come out of this Puzzle Town.

Where shall we go? I said.
   Outside the city limits
Lie the farms of dread   *40*
   Stocked with fear herds and bite crops.

There's a lake—we'll swim in it,
    Said Seth with a flourish.
There's a tree, we'll sit under it.
    He blew a trumpet.

Now the lake was Milky Way's
    Underpettiwhirlyworld,
And the tree, so my friend says,
    Was Grandfather's old cane.

Then up sprang Uncle and Aunt Good and Evil.   50
    They came out at us screaming:
Stop that fornicating
    In the bushes with that milkywaymaid.

We see no wrong, did we sing back,
    No rampant rogues, no slut,
Nothing but
Time crossing space, planet tree and milky lake.

The tree looked at itself in the water,
    We bent it down in the milky depth;
        A seven-oared boat   60
Discovered the elusive daughter.

We sang out with crucified jewsharps.
    Aunt and Uncle turned into gate posts,
We sang in wooden flats and naily sharps,
    The Yard went into the House.

Seth said: "Swallow the stone he gave you!"
    I did and behold these marvellous things:
Abel flew by like a mile high killdeer
    With six wings.

Cain turned into his thistly nest,   70
    Puzzle Town solved itself,
The Farm tipped back at last
    And my Father mended.

A sky of cloudy breasts
    Rained milk:
The blood of a giant heart
    Pounded beneath my crystal raft.

There was nothing left but the killdeer,
    He skated the cold spring air
Over the old pasture, the line of elms,   80
    The Easter farmhouse, I there

        Heard his cry
And saw all vanish into him:
All time, all Space, all Bible
    Into that giant stormy die.

1965

SELECTIONS FROM TWELVE LETTERS TO A SMALL TOWN- 1962

✻ FIRST LETTER

To the Avon River above Stratford, Canada

What did the Indians call you?
For you do not flow
With English accents.
I hardly know
What I should call you
    Because before
I drank coffee or tea
    I drank you
    With my cupped hands
And you did not taste English to me   10
    And you do not sound
    Like Avon
    Or swans & bards
But rather like the sad wild fowl
    In prints drawn
    By Audubon
And like dear bad poets
    Who wrote
    Early in Canada
And never were of note.   20
You are the first river
    I crossed
And like the first whirlwind
    The first rainbow
    First snow, first
    Falling star I saw,
You, for other rivers are my law.
    These other rivers:
    The Red & the Thames
    Are never so sweet   30
To skate upon, swim in
    Or for baptism of sin.
    Silver and light

The sentence of your voice,
  With a soprano
Continuous cry you shall
  Always flow
  Through my heart.
The rain and the snow of my mind
Shall supply the spring of that river   40
  Forever.
Though not your name
Your coat of arms I know
      And motto:
A shield of reeds and cresses
  Sedges, crayfishes
The hermaphroditic leech
Minnows, muskrats and farmers' geese
And printed above this shield
One of my earliest wishes   50
"To flow like you."

★ *FIFTH LETTER*

The Cloakroom at the High School

The high school is the palace of Merlin and Cheiron
  Where governors and governesses teach
The young Achilles and young Arthurs of the town.

The radiators teach the rule of monotony
  Cheep cheep cheeping in the winter classroom
Timid fingers learn to turn a fire on.

A stuffed hummingbird and a stuffed sandhill crane.
  In the dusty looking glass of grammar,
Number, the young see the shape of their brain.

But what and where did I learn most from?   10
High, dark, narrow as its single window
In the old high school there was a cloakroom—

A cloakroom! In winter stuffed with cloaks
  Soft with outside things inside
Burs, mud, dead leaves on some of the coats.

At four o'clock there are forty-nine bare hooks
   As a hundred hands reach up
And I, lingering rearranging my books

See sweeping face peer in of janitor
   Alone in the winter twilight
The old janitor! An image to ponder over.   20

Of course I learnt snow dripping windows
   Corridors of words, cobwebs of character,
The ninety-two elements in a long row,
            But most I learnt

The insoluble mystery of the cloakroom
   And the curious question of the janitor
      In some way so centre and core
            January man and cloakroom
From which the moon each month unlocks upon the wave
   A white bird.   30

✸ TWELFTH LETTER

The Bicycle

Halfway between childhood & manhood,
   More than a hoop but never a car,
The bicycle talks gravel and rain pavement
   On the highway where the dead frogs are.

Like sharkfish the cars blur by,
   Filled with the two-backed beast
One dreams of, yet knows not the word for,
   The accumulating sexual yeast.

Past the house where the bees winter,
  I climb on the stairs of my pedals
To school murmuring irregular verbs
  Past the lion with legs like a table's.

Autumn blows the windfalls down
  With a twilight horn of dead leaves.
I pick them up in the fence of November
  And burs on my sweater sleeves.

Where a secret robin is wintering
  By the lake in the fir grove dark
Through the fresh new snow we stumble
  That Winter has whistled sharp.

The March wind blows me ruts over,
  Puddles past, under red maple buds,
Over culvert of streamling, under
  White clouds and beside bluebirds.

Fireflies tell their blinking player
  Piano hesitant tales
Down at the bridge through the swamp
  Where the ogre clips his rusty nails.

Between the highschool & the farmhouse
  In the country and the town
It was a world of love and of feeling
  Continually floating down

On a soul whose only knowledge
  Was that everything was something,
This was like that, that was like this—
    In short, everything was
    The bicycle of which I sing.

TWO EMBLEMS 1969

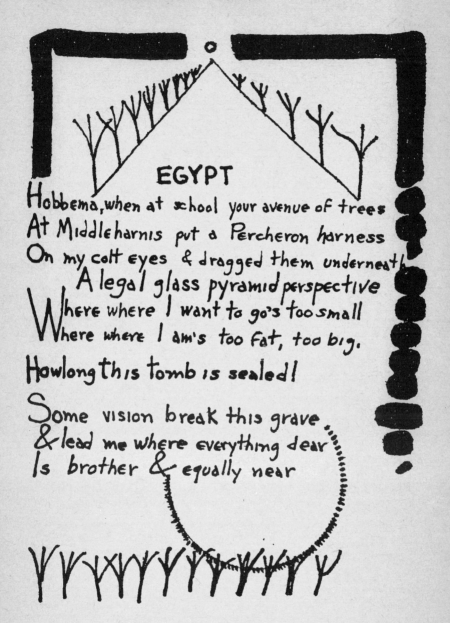

EGYPT

Hobbema, when at school your avenue of trees
At Middleharnis put a Percheron harness
On my colt eyes & dragged them underneath
    A legal glass pyramid perspective
Where where I want to go's too small
Where where I am's too fat, too big.

Howlong this tomb is sealed!

Some vision break this grave
& lead me where everything dear
Is brother & equally near

The TREE

A record when a tree's cut down?
A stone thrown into a pond?
No,   planets orbiting our sun.

Yes, night-sky's a forest.
Each tree has a star core.

Once before I woke I reached
A path where you can touch
Our rough furrowed skin & bark

Inside which rind we sleeping are.

SOME DRAMATIC VERSE 1958-71

From "The Killdeer" (second version), Act II :
The River of Time

[The scene is the late Mrs. Gardner's deserted cottage. The two old women are cleaning up.]

Mrs. Budge
  Oh, the river of time, the river of time,
  The clouds of the moments, the clouds of the moments,
  Clouds of escaping birds from the dark barn.
  I grab here, I grab there, birds you escape me.
  The wind of the hours, wind of the hours,
  The snow of the minutes, snow of the minutes,
  It all falls into the river of time and is swept away.

Mrs. Delta
  Oh, the river of time, the river of time.

Mrs. Budge
  What am I to dust now? Those curlicues
  On the stove? No, you couldn't have done them,
  Mrs. Delta, I could plant them with seeds.
  Just look, Mrs. Delta.

Mrs. Delta
  I ain't done nothing but mop round that stove,
  Mrs. Budge. I mopped, and I mop.

1960, 1968

From the Radio Collage "Canada Dash, Canada Dot"
Part II : The Line Up and Down

Yonge Street

Man
   Existence waked me here on this cement tapeworm
     Called Yonge Street
   Take a step, take a breath, take a step, take a breath
     This day and every day
     Called Yonge Street
   I can remember the tokens that made it all go
     Eliza Regina Imperatrix
   It was a sort of weather in your pocket
   I can remember a fishhead at Savarin's Grill
   The crowds of other-me's walked above the rush   10
   Beneath them lakeward of their own sewerage

Girl
   By the way, where is the golden branch I gave you?

Man
   A cunning Melinda Street boss ate it like a candy stick
   He wore a gray suit and had bellies under his eyes.

Girl
   And where is the silver cup and grail we gave you?
Man
   A paper King Street woman with instalments for eyes
   And typewriters for feet--she pawned it.
   But I have here instead this long gray vertebrae
   The backbone of a city; my backbone as a matter of fact.
   Now that I'm dead   20
   Will it do instead
   Of the golden branch and the silver cup
   I was given when
   First I journeyed to the world of men?

1958, 1966

From "Listen to the Wind", Act II
"Lock up your doors and pen your flocks"

Chorus
> Lock up your doors and pen your flocks,
>   A storm comes with the night,
> The stars go out and the windows latch,
>   Babies cry out in fright.
>
> Over the hills and under the sky
>   The huntsman and his hounds,
> The huntsman's dark and 12 feet high —
>   Hear him galloping by.
>
> His dogs gnash in their kennels of skull
>   And now he lets them out,   10
> His dogs of rage and his wolves of blood
>   Raise a dreadful shout
>
> Over the hills and under the sky
>   The huntsman and his hounds.
> He rides the wind with a dreadful cry
>   And Hell itself comes nigh.
>
> Closer they come. Have you shut the door?
>   What have you left outside,
> His horse must eat. Leave out a thing.
>   He will not be denied.   20
>
> Over the hills and under the sky
>   The huntsman and his hounds —
> "Have you blood for us and any bones?"
>   Hear their thrilling cry!
>
> We've left a last sheaf in the field.
>   Huntsman it is for you.
> Take it and leave ourselves unharmed.
>   And do not us pursue.
>
> Over the hills and under the sky
>   Over the hills and under the sky   30
>   Over the hills and under the sky
>   Over the hills and under the sky.

1966

From "Colours in the Dark", two "pyramids":
    Scene 8: Berry Picking

[*Bear runs off with child, kids enter shrieking*]

Kids
  A bear ran off with Sadie! A bear ran off with
  Sadie! And it takes a lot of people to produce
  one child.

[*They form a family tree pyramid with a reappearing Sadie.*]

Kids
                    It takes
                  Two parents
               Four Grandparents
            Eight Great grandparents
        Sixteen Great great grandparents
     Thirty-two Great great great grandparents
  Sixty-four Great great great great grandparents   10
One hundred and twenty-eight Great great great great great
                    grandparents
Two hundred and fifty-six Great great great great great great
                    grandparents
Five hundred and twelve Great great great great great great
                  great grandparents
One thousand and twenty-four Great great great great great great
                great great grandparents

[*It would take over a thousand people to do this scene: at Listeners'
Workshop we did it with thirty-two people: the children here
suggested—by a triangle arrangement, the thousand ancestors behind
each human being. Have one group of players in charge of chanting
"Great great" & "grandparents".*]

Sadie
  Are you there 1,024 ancestors?

[*a feeble rustle*]

  Are you there 512
  Are you there 256
  Are you there 128

[*sound gets louder, less ghost-like and more human*]

  Are you there 64
  Are you there 32   20
  Are you there 16

[More recent ancestors step forward and say firmly and clearly what
we have only dimly heard: "We're here."]

Are you there 8
Are you there 4
Are you there Mother and Father?

[Gramp, Ma and Pa step forward and establish the next scene as the
kids fade away.]

Scene 21 : The Bridge

... OR EVEN ADOLF HITLER HAD 1024 GREAT GREAT GREAT GREAT
GREAT GREAT GREAT GREAT GRANDPARENTS AND KEPT A PLAY
BOX TOO.

[Father speaks, Son acts out situation for him.]

Pa
On one of my walks—I came to a river. There
was a bridge. But under the bridge there was
a swan. He hissed at me. I couldn't cross.

[Set this up as a bridge with something white under it. A girl with long
white glove as the swan's neck. The situation—the entire company
crosses the bridge, but the hero can't. On the other side they beckon to
him silently, but he won't cross.]

I can't cross. I'm afraid! I was like one of
those people you hear about in mental hospitals
Who can't go through a doorway.

The pebble is a huge dark hill I must climb   10
The dewdrop is a great storm lake that we must cross
The string is a road that I cannot find
The straw is a sign whose meaning I forget
      Hill   Lake   Road   Sign

[The Bear chases him to the middle of the bridge. A tug of war between
the people and the Bear helped by Lady Death. He is pulled
across—perhaps loses something. The Bear and Lady Death dispute
over this—with some other sinister figures who gather. Lady Death is
played by Grandmother. They fade and the cast form the family tree
pyramid; the Stage turns slowly yellow.]

All

It Takes
The Remembering
Of   four   seasons
Eight   Stars
Sixteen   Sunsets
Thirty-Two   Wind whistles   20
Sixty-four   Dewdrops in the sunrise
One hundred and twenty-eight   Trembling leaves
Two hundred and fifty-six   Pebbles
Five hundred and twelve   Snowflakes
One thousand and twenty-four   Cloud shadows
To make one soul

[The family tree pyramid now reverses so it is an arrow pointing at a child standing on the trestles. This child turns his face. He is masked and dressed as Adolf Hitler.
SCREEN: Swastika.
We hear a Nazi children's song and the roar of a Nuremberg rally. All file off, Father helping the Hitler boy down and off.]

1967

From "Sticks and Stones"
   The case against Donnelly,
   and Jennie's dawn-song at the wake

[The scene is the wake for the Donnellys. We shift back and forth in time as Mrs. Donnelly tells her son Will about their troubles, and the grown-up Jennie and Will comment on what happened. The "clappers" are the Donnelly's friends, the "stampers" their enemies.]

Mrs. Donnelly
   One night, Will, your father was up the road visiting a farmer he was to do some work for the next morning. They followed him there.
Stampers
   Come out Jim Donnelly
Mrs. Donnelly
   They said to your father.
First Stamper
   Put on you my good fellow and come out till two or three of your neighbours that wish you well gets a sight of your purty face you babe of grace.
Mrs. Donnelly
   Your father kept quiet. So they say.
Stampers
   Open up in the Queen's name, Jim Donnelly. We've a warrant for your arrest.
Mrs. Donnelly
   Your father stood behind the door and he says
Mr. Donnelly
   Who are you that wants me at all.
Mrs. Donnelly
   and they says
Stampers
   Come out first avourneen.
Mrs. Donnelly
   He opened the door and came out.
Stampers
   Jim Donnelly. The Whitefeet hear that you let one of your mares stand to Sealey's entire horse last Monday coming home from the fair.
Mrs. Donnelly
   To which your father replied

Mr. Donnelly
   [*at back stage where the crowd has been focussing*] It was love at
   first sight. Shure Sealey's stallion was mounting my one mare before I
   could stop him. I had my back turned at the time just for the merest
   minute getting my other mare's tail disentangled from a thornbush.
Stampers
   Did you not know no Whitefoot is to have any dealings with the
   Protestant and the heretic Sealey?
Mr. Donnelly
   Yes, but it was
Stampers
   Kneel, Donnelly. Get down on your knees.

[*But he stands. A barrel is rolled back and forth a bit in the crowd.*]

First Stamper
   Swear [*striking a book*] that you will not withdraw yourself from this
   society — the Whitefeet [*candles*].
Mr. Donnelly
   But you see I won't kneel. And I won't swear.
Second Stamper
   If you refuse [*the barrel is rolled around*] if you refuse, Donnelly, you
   won't know the day nor the hour nor the [*light stamping rhythm
   repeated*]
Mr. Donnelly
   No, I'm not.
First Stamper
   Kneel.
Mr. Donnelly
   No.
First Stamper
   Swear.
Mr. Donnelly
   No! I won't kneel.
Mrs. Donnelly
   So they cursed your father and called him a
All
   Blackfoot!

[*The barrel is rolled off to some secret end.*]

Mrs. Donnelly
    Isn't today your birthday Will? Go over to that old tree the storm fell
    down and see what you find hidden in among the roots.
The Boy Will
    A fiddle. Is it for my birthday, Mother?
Mrs. Donnelly
    It's for your life, Will. Anybody that talks of Whitefeet and Blackfeet
    in Canada here is nothing but bullies and blowhards. We showed
    them in Ireland and we'll show them here in Canada. What does your
    father care if they've followed him. After the harvest he'll own this
    ground we stand on and the fields he's made. You'll see — they'll try
    to drive us off, Will.
All
    A high gray hill   That's Keeper's Hill   ash trees
Mrs. Donnelly
    But here we'll stay
All
    Thorn tree   blackbird flying close   far
    farther   farthest   away
Mrs. Donnelly
    If you're afraid you should be
Stampers
    Ireland
Mrs. Donnelly
    If you're not   you'll live
Clappers
    Ireland
Mrs. Donnelly
    Ireland. Old names — Blackfoot! Whitefoot! Slavery.
    Canada's a new fiddle, Will, and we're free.
Stampers
    [*softly as the mother and son mingle with the chorus*]   Ireland
Jennie
    And that is why, mother, they burnt you
Clappers
    First with their tongues

Jennie
        then with their kerosene
Because you were tall, you were different
        and you weren't afraid
Be not afraid now at the thorn apple fields
Stampers
    Stars above   clouds below and snow still around
    Mourning till dawn from midnight to dawn
    A bone for Jennie and a fiddle for Will
    Four stones where there once was a home
    Five dead people have come to this house
Jennie
    I help my mother cross the thorn apple fields
    We pay you toll with our thoughts and tears
The Man Will
    Requiem aeternam dona eis, Domine, et lux perpetua luceat eis.
Jennie
    Cum sanctus tuis in aeternum, quia pius es
The Man Will
    For at dawn comes a sleigh
Jennie
    To bear you away
    For awhile from us
    As we mourn in this house
    The last tollgate before harvest and heaven.

1971

INDEX TO TITLES

INDEX TO FIRST LINES